First Prayers

by Helen Gompertz
illustrated by Vic Mitchell

Contents

Judson Press® Valley Forge

Prayers about me

Thank you, God,
that you made me.
I think sometimes that
I look best in my
new clothes, but
thank you, God,
because you love me
always, even when
my clothes are old
and torn, or I have got
muddy when I played
outside.

Thank you, God, for my eyes.
When I am happy, they sparkle.
When I am sad, they fill with tears.
Sometimes when I am angry,
they look angry, too.
I can use them to see all the wonderful
things in the world around me. I can see the
birds and the trees, the sea and the
cliffs, the traffic in the street.
Thank you, God, for giving me eyes to see
your beautiful world.

Thank you, God, for giving me hands
with fingers.
I wonder, why did you think of ten?
They help me to count.
They help me to hold things.
They help me to touch and feel.
I can hold hands with my friends.
But sometimes I grab things instead of
waiting my turn. I am sorry.
Sometimes I use my hands to punch or
push, instead of helping other people.
I am sorry, God.

Thank you, God, for my legs which help me to run far and fast.

Thank you, God, for giving me such strong legs. I see babies who have only short fat little legs. They can only kick their legs in the air, but I can play and jump and run.

My brother fell over and cut his knee today. Please help him to be brave and make his knee better soon.

Thank you, God, for my nose.
Thank you for the smell of the bubbles in
my bath and my toothpaste.
Thank you for all the good smells from the
kitchen where the food is cooked.
Thank you for the scent of flowers.
Thank you for the smells which warn me of
danger, like gas or burning.

Thank you, God, that I can taste
when I eat.
I like the taste of ice cream and cookies.
I like the taste of salty nuts and sweet
lollipops.
I like . . . *(here the child may insert
        some favorite tastes)*
I don't always like the tastes that grown-ups
enjoy, but thank you for making me able to taste.

Thank you, God, for bedtime.
Sometimes I don't feel like going to bed but
I like it when Mommy and Daddy read stories
to me. I like the fun of bathtimes.
I like the feel of clean sheets and warm
quilts and I love to snuggle down with my
teddies and toys.

Thank you for the little light
that shines in the dark in my bedroom.
Mommy says that day and night are all the same
to you.
Thank you that you never fall asleep. Please
take care of me while I am asleep tonight.
Good night, Lord Jesus.

Dear God, some days are sad.
I get up and there are big gray clouds
outside in the sky and I feel dreary inside
myself.
Sometimes my Mommy looks glum and my
Daddy looks sad.
Please help us to cheer up so that we can
smile and laugh again.

Oh God, the sun is shining and I
feel like singing at the top of my voice.
The world is a happy place today.
Help me to make other people
happy, too. Dear God, there are
lots of sad people
in the world today.
Please help me
to remember
them.

Prayers about my family

Dear God, I am happy because I
love my Mommy and Daddy.
Thank you for all the people who love me,
as well as all the people I love: younger
brothers and sisters—even when they pull
my hair or wake Mommy and Daddy in the night.
My friends—even when they don't want to share
with me.
My uncles and aunts, grandmas and grandpas.
Thank you that there is plenty of love to
go around for everyone in the family.

Dear Lord Jesus,
Daddy was cross today because I
wouldn't come when I was called. He says
he still loves me even when I'm naughty
and I know you do, too.
Sorry, God.

*This prayer can be used when friends
are having problems in their families:*

Dear Lord, Jesus, I just don't understand
it—my friend says that her Mommy doesn't
love her Daddy anymore.
You help us all to love one another. Please
help that family to love again.

Dear Lord Jesus, my brother is ill and my Mommy has been nursing him all day. It is hard not to feel left out, but please help me to understand.

Dear Lord Jesus, Grandma is coming to stay with us today. She is gentle and kind. She tells me about things my Daddy did when he was little like I am. She brings me books and reads me stories. I love her, but she does not like noise. Please help us to be quiet enough for her.

Dear God, I went for a walk with Grandpa today. I have to walk slowly to keep back with him. Sometimes he seems to be very tired. Please take care of him because I love him very much.

Dear Lord Jesus, my Uncle and Aunt are coming to stay with us. They will bring all my cousins and we shall play together. Thank you for cousins and uncles and aunts. Please give us a good time together.

Dear Lord Jesus,
We've got a new baby—
I'm sure he's going to be fun later—
but now—
He can't play football.
He hasn't any teeth.
His hands are so tiny.
He cries a lot.
Will he break if I drop him?
Why does he only sleep and why
does everyone stop to look at him?
—I want to understand—
He's my new baby brother.
Please help me to love him.

Lord Jesus, my Aunt is coming to see me today. She is special and talks to you about me nearly every day. Thank you for giving me special people to help look after me.

Dear God, thank you for brothers and sisters. I am sorry when I quarrel with them, or when I grumble when they stay up later than I do. I am sorry, God.

*Often children encounter bereavement in
their lives, particularly in regard to
grandparents, uncles, and aunts. This may
be useful then, with appropriate changes:*

Dear God, my Grandma is lonely because
Grandpa has died. She has no one to take care
of her now.
No one to take her to church.
No one to talk with at breakfast.
No one to look after her.
Please, will you help—I know you take
special care of lonely people.

Dear Lord Jesus, I have so many friends and such a happy family.
Please help me to make friends with lonely people. I could visit them and talk. I could paint a picture or make a design, or my Mommy or Daddy could take them out in the car with us.
Help me to be a friend to lonely people.

Prayers about my home

Dear Lord, thank you that I have a house to live in. Thank you that when I come home from school or play, it feels warm and welcomes me. Thank you that I can find my books and toys here and this is where I really feel safe and happy.

Dear God, my Daddy has been doing
some work in the house today. He told me a story
about Joseph while he was doing it.
He told me Joseph worked with a hammer, nails, and
wood.
I guess you, Jesus, must have
watched Joseph work,
I watched my Daddy today.

Dear God, thank you for the
kitchen in my house.
I love to see
my Mommy rolling out
the pastry and to smell the
cakes and pies as they cook in
the oven.
I like to feel that I can help my
Mommy, too. Please help me
with all my jobs and Mommy
with her bigger ones.

Dear Lord Jesus, we are moving tomorrow. Mommy says the new house is bigger and it will have more room for my toys.

Please take care of me in the new house, especially when I feel a bit scared.

Please help me not to feel afraid if it seems so empty or smells different, or seems too big, or too small.

(Here a child may like to add his or her suggestions about what might frighten him or her about the move.)

Please help me in all this not to feel afraid. Thank you for taking care of me always.

Note: If you live in a town or city, you may want to substitute flowerpots or window boxes for the word garden, and plants for potatoes.

Lord Jesus, I planted some seeds in my garden today and Daddy put in some potatoes. I made a hole with my finger, I popped in the seed, then covered it with a blanket of earth, then I gave it a drink of water.
I can't wait to see if it has any roots.
I can't wait to see if it has a leaf or a shoot.
I feel like digging it up just to see—but no, Daddy says not to. Thank you, God, for my seed.

Thank you, God, for the apartments in our building. The roof at the top seems to reach to the sky and it's hard work getting up all the stairs when you only have little legs.
Thank you, God, for elevators.
They creak and groan and bump.
They seem to swallow you up.
They sometimes seem to shake.
But they do get you up to the top of the stairs.

Thank you, God,
for the street where I live.
Thank you for all the front doors
of different colors. I like
to walk on top of the little
wall in front of some of the
houses, but sometimes
people get cross
and I have to jump down fast.
What fun it is to
be tall on a wall
and not fall!

Thank you, God, for the street where I
live, the lampposts with the lights at night,
and the cans where we can put all our rubbish.
Thank you, God, for the street
where I live.

Thank you, God, for roofs. When I
look out of my bedroom
window, I see roofs and roofs and roofs.
Some are gray.
Some are black.
Some are sloping.
Some are flat.
Some are made of glass.
Thank you for roofs. They keep out the rain;
they shade us from the sun when it
shines. I like to watch the birds when they
hop along the roofs or when they just
perch on top.

Prayers about my pets

I like pets.
I like cats and kittens with soft fur
and the purring noises they make
when they are happy. But I don't like
their claws or their spitting when they
feel cross. Still, I'm sure they don't
like it if I shout or get rough.

I like dogs and puppies with their
floppy ears, cold wet noses, and wagging
tails. But I don't like it when
they chew my books and toys or bark
too loudly. Still, I'm sure they don't
like it if I tire them by throwing their ball too
far or try to carry them around.

I like rabbits with their pink eyes,
soft silky ears, and cotton ball
tails. But I don't like it when they get out and
eat our lettuce or trample over the flower beds.
Still, I'm sure they don't like it when I
forget to feed them or clean their
hutches.

I like pets—please help me to
care for them always with love.

25

Thank you, God, for
hamsters with their babies
and their pouches.
I get tired of doing the same thing
for very long but they don't.
They go around and around on the wheel
in their cage or seem quite happy just
eating and sleeping.

Thank you, God, for tropical fish
with bright colors—vivid blues, greens,
orange, red. Some dart about the tank in
quick sharp moves.
Some swim lazily around, gazing out at
the world outside.
I like fish—they are like people:
some are busy; some are slow.
Thank you, God, because you made each of
us different.

Thank you, God, for parakeets —their feathers are such lovely bright colors, and they chirp so cheerfully. They like looking at themselves in the little mirrors they have in their cages. Sometimes we can let them out to fly around the room. Then there's a flurry of feathers, and a swoop and a dive. But soon all is quiet, for they know they're safer in the cage.

I like to take my dog for a walk.
I like to throw sticks in the field and watch
him dash madly to fetch them.
I like to see him scratching and digging to
uncover who knows what.
A bone he has buried?
A favorite stick?
A long-lost treasure like a ball half chewed?
Thank you, God, for dogs.
They really seem such good friends to us.

Prayers for when I'm out and about

Dear Lord Jesus, a supermarket is such
a very big place; there is so much noise—
people chattering, music playing—
I can hardly hear what Mommy says to me.
There are so many big piles of cans,
of packets, and of boxes.
If I pulled one, the whole pile would come
tumbling down.
There are funny smells—
of bacon,
of cheese,
and of bread baking.
Thank you, Lord, for supermarkets.

Dear God, you have to look after
a world full of people, yet Mommy says you
take special care of me.
When I'm in a crowd,
the grown-ups seem so tall
and I am only small.
My hands get tired of reaching up for theirs.
Their shopping bags catch in my hair.
Sometimes when they talk to one another
they forget me, and when I'm so far down
beneath them they can't hear what I say.
Thank you that you can always hear when
I talk to you, wherever I am.
Thank you, God.

Thank you, God, for buses.
I like red and green ones, or bright blue
ones. I like to look out the high windows—
look down on people's heads, their hats, or their
umbrellas in the rain.
I like to give the driver my money, or drop it
in the box. I like to pull the cord to
tell the driver to stop.
I like buses.
Thank you, God, for all
the drivers—please keep them safe.

Thank you, God, for the garages that
have lots of floors.
They look like car sandwiches.
I wonder if we shall remember where we left
our car,
but Daddy always seems to know.

Thank you, God, for trains and busy
stations.
Thank you for all the machines where
I can get candy or gum.
Thank you for the subway trains in the
city.
Please help me always to do what Mommy says
so I can be safe.

Thank you, God, for giant road sweepers
and the garbage trucks.
It would be so dirty on the roads without
them.
Thank you for the drivers and the workers.

© Scripture Union 1980
Judson Press Edition 1983
Third Printing 1988
All rights reserved
Judson Press is registered as a trademark
in the U.S. Patent Office
Printed in Great Britain by Ebenezer Baylis & Son Limited, Worcester and London